I0829215

I WANNA MAKE JAZZ TO YOU

TEXTS BY MOE SEAGER
ARTWORK BY LEÏLA CHAIX

Published in Oxford by The Onslaught Pre
11 Ridley Road, OX4 2(
September, 20

Edited by Mathew Staunt
Copy Editor: Charlotte Rieg

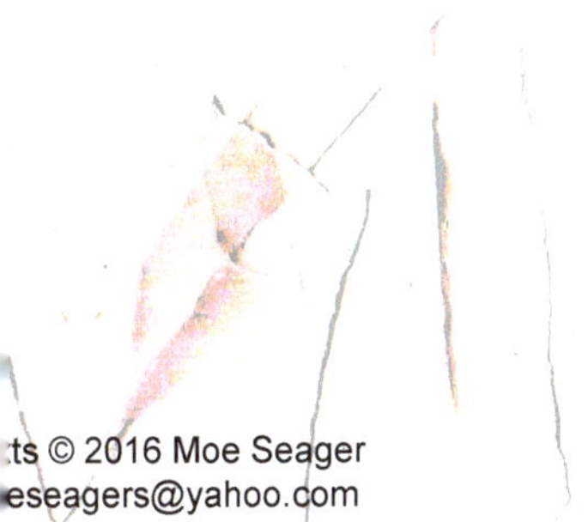

eseagers@yahoo.com

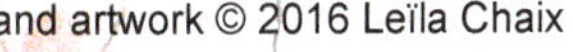

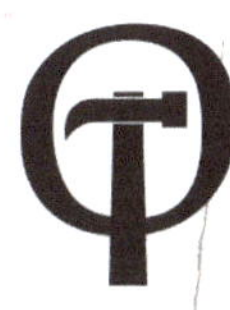

3N 978-0-9956225-1-7

eset in Arial and Gobold & designed by Leïla Chaix

anks to Lindsay A. Gordon for production support

you.

Bite me Bitch

RED

4 A.M.

5 A.M.

Mantilla

Suite in Three Movements

Oblivion Magic

Your Kiss

Sylvia's Song

Perhaps

I wanna make Jazz to you

Wasted Time at the Bookstore

Blue Bonnet Girl

The Engagement

Baby's Lust

The Wake

Seductress

Dugan and Reilly

Valentine's Oracle

HERE

BITE
ME
BITCH

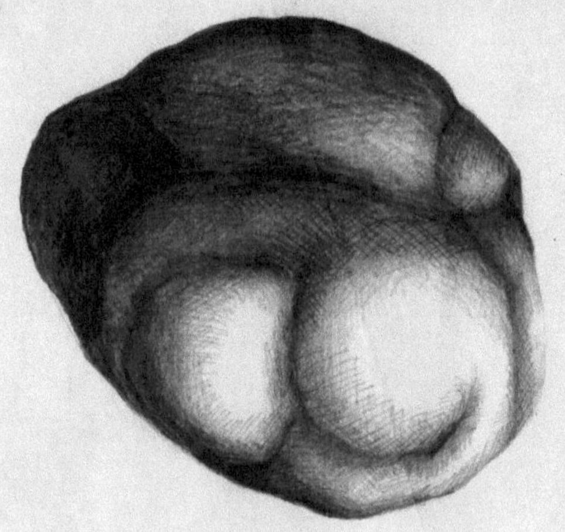

I have a thing about biting
Biting people to stay alive
Biting made the little boys cry
I masticate on red meat
Enter me, make a pact
Bite me Bitch

Go to a pocket of flesh
Tongue me like a knife
Wet me down, cut me up
Take me to the razor edge
Incise me with your fangs
I will come like a free verb
Bite me Bitch

Plunge into my neck
Dive deep and sink
Pierce my thigh with your sharpened nail
Rip me like an article of faith
A dripping covenant
Bite me Bitch

I'll take you by your knotted hair
Your excited limbs flail wildly
Like two hungry canines
Stalking for the blood
We howl, we fill the empty night
Bite, bite, bite

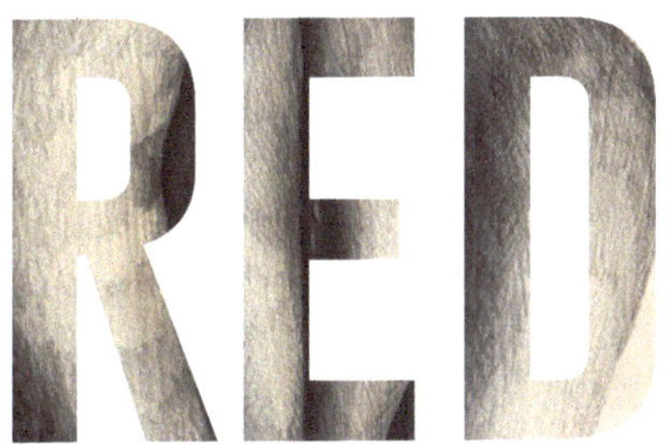
RED

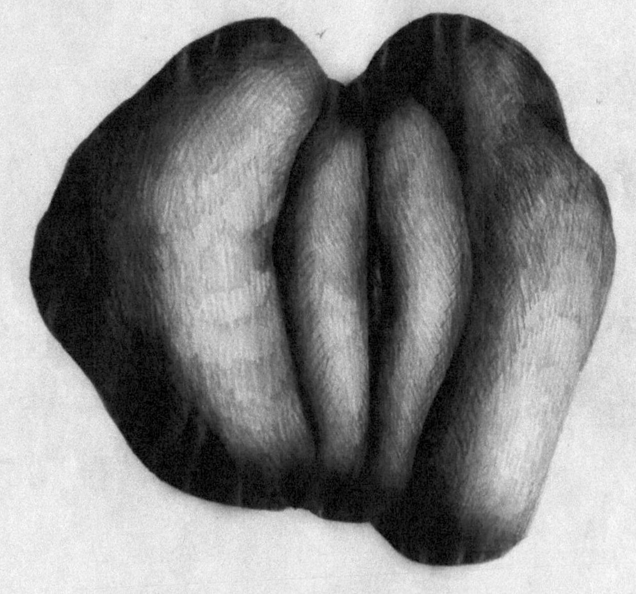

I come upon a tooth brush red
Lying on the sink, bristles up, spread
Below the mirror, yours, it is wet
Lifting it to my mouth, I plunge
Eyes closed, I suck it
A long wet minute

Turn it over and around, slippery friction
In my mouth up and down, I rub
Against my gums your moist brush rouge
Flush to my lips I spread
A white paste oozing from a stiff white tube

This mix discharges sweet sensations
To my taste buds agitated for
Your faint liquid trace, so good I
Need to swallow, to gulp
Deep down, down deep it fills
The empty hole in my . . .

Tongue to your delicate instrument
Intimate, I ebb and flow, boundaries melt
Grip firm, fix, release
When it all comes, together, dabs and drops
Dripping from the corner of my . . .
Why did I open my eyes

4 A.M.

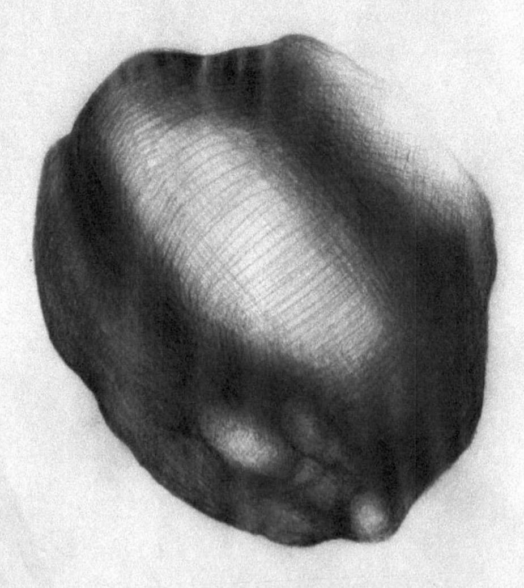

We arrived at your place, it was very late
I on a second wind, you on a blind date
Anxious moments, the vein in my neck
I was hard and you were wet
Sweat and perfume
The air was heavy

You took my tongue
Sucked like an artichoke heart
I ran fingers through your hair
Cleaving creases on the back on your neck
Jungle cats on a mating call

Drawn deeper, swollen as it was
Sliding down the ravenous oval made of your mouth
Gums throbbing, lips dripping
Finger sheathed in sugarous saliva
Mere touch your nipple rose like a buoy
Porous brown bobbing atop ivory breast

Magnetic charge in a rapturous storm
Hot stake rising from quivering thighs
Lava rush about to spew

Taking three, deep, slow breaths
Plunging the tongue for more
Second time good
As the first

5 A.M.

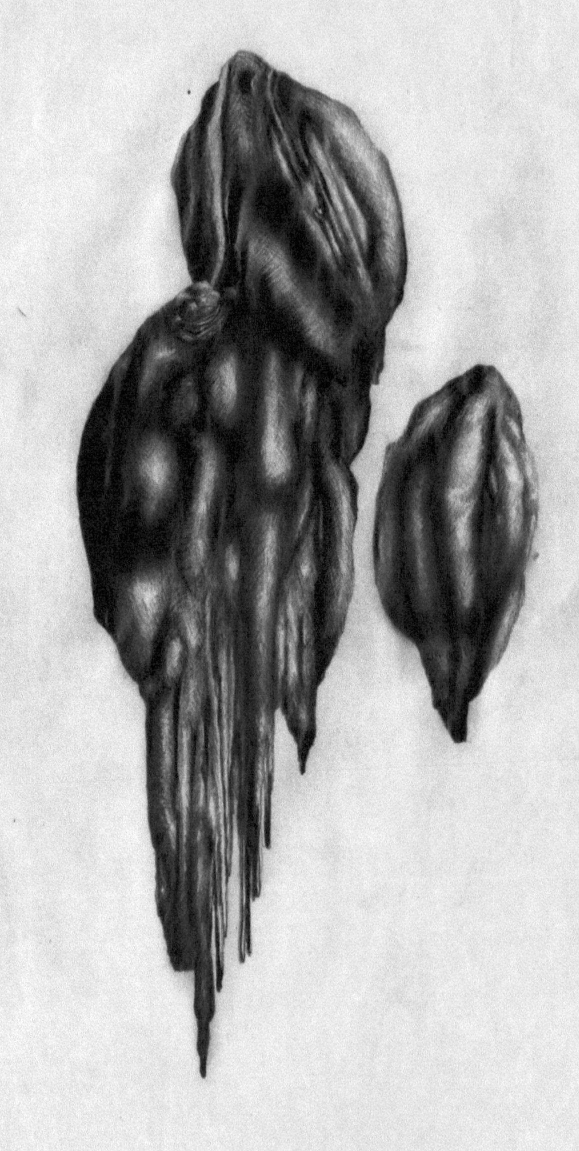

*Laid in a pocket between darkness and dawn,
city shit mates with lipstick and spent sweat on
the cushion you rest your head upon at her place
she hands you a broken cigarette you light off the
burner on the stove. It's 5 a.m. over Boulevard
Magenta in a tree across the rue pigeon squawk at
2 crows fighting like cats and dogs, rats drag away
the pizza with pepperoni dropped on the sidewalk
wetted red in wino piss. A woman steps by in
shoes that kill you would marry her in a New York
minute just to kiss her breathless lips and walk
beside her in that dress shapely as you ever
desired. She asks, ça va chérie? Oui babe, play
me 'Les Feuilles Mortes' and we surrender to
carnal knowledge, put asleep by the hiss of the
number 9 metro.*

** 'Les Feuilles Mortes' (Autumn Leaves), 1949—a French song written by poet Jacques Prévert and composed by Joseph Kosma*

(mantilla: a silk or lace head scarf clipped to a comb on the back of a woman's head so as to drape her shoulders and back. Traditionally worn by Spanish and Mexican women.)

MANTIL-

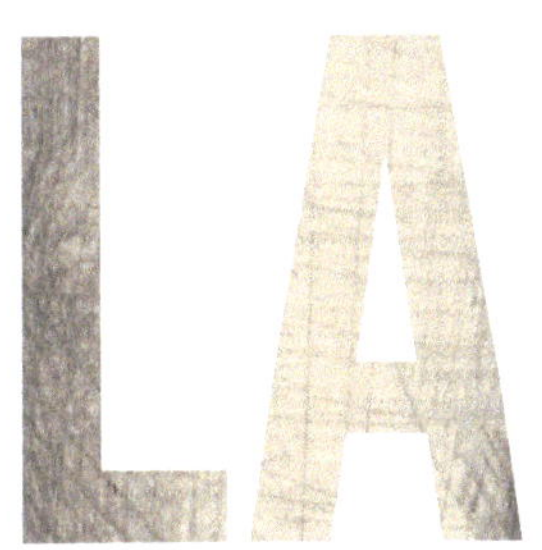

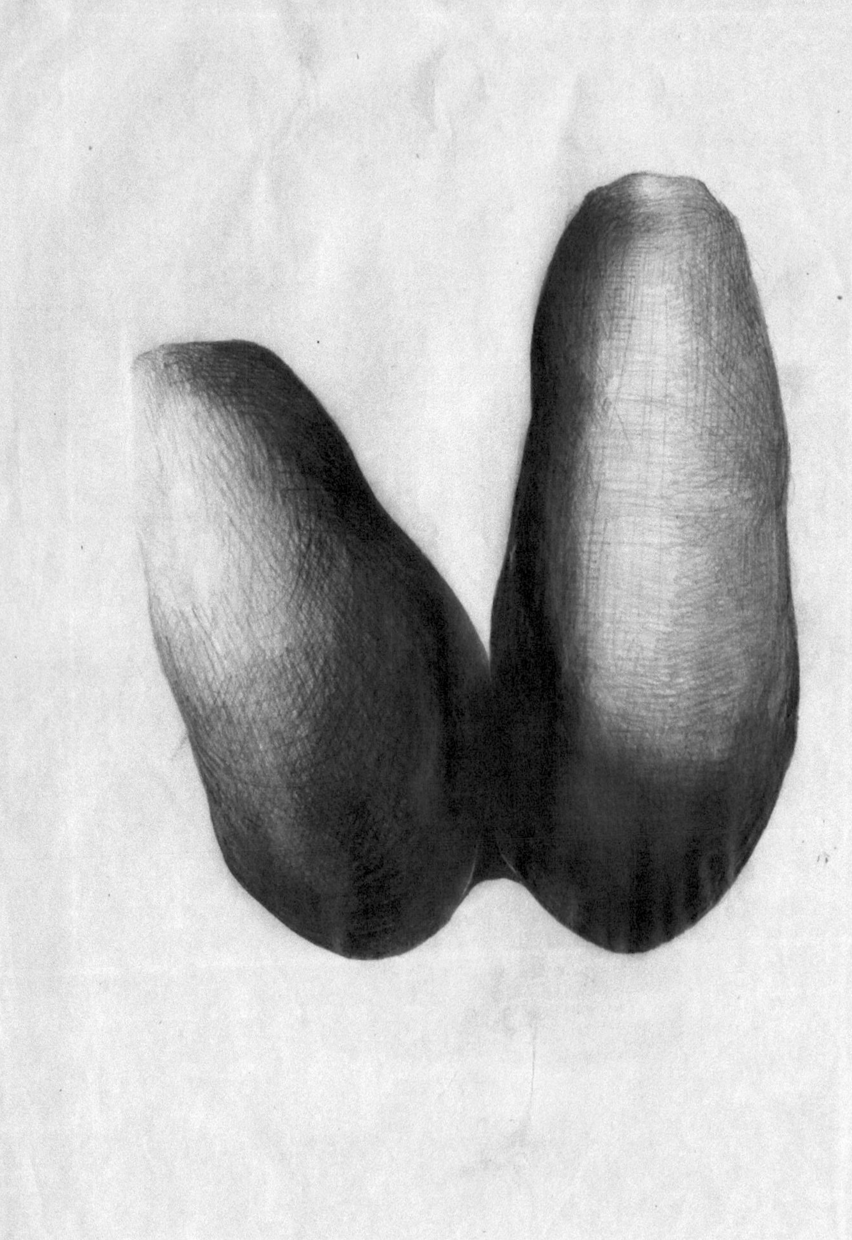

Isabel came to dinner
All in black and feline gray
Her Spanish accent thick and wet
A glass of wine, dark bordeaux
The color of her lips

Isabel came to dinner
She lit a pink cigarette
I watched the ashes fall
Into a porcelain cup
I watched her brush her teeth
With a sweep of her tongue

Isabel came to dinner
Alone
She wandered through the room
Her chestnut eyes, slits half closed
Low fires burning, those eyes
Moonlight under water

Isabel came to dinner
She stayed late
Tossing our voices back and forth
We mixed our words
Uhm . . . in the key of G
Tango in the sitting room

Isabel came to dinner
She rose in midnight leather boots
I expected a mantilla
She laughed in my face
Taunted, I whispered, shall we go?
Later, a candle burning
The sleeping rose

SUITE IN THREE MOVE- MENTS

1.

INTAN-GIBLE LAW OF LOVE

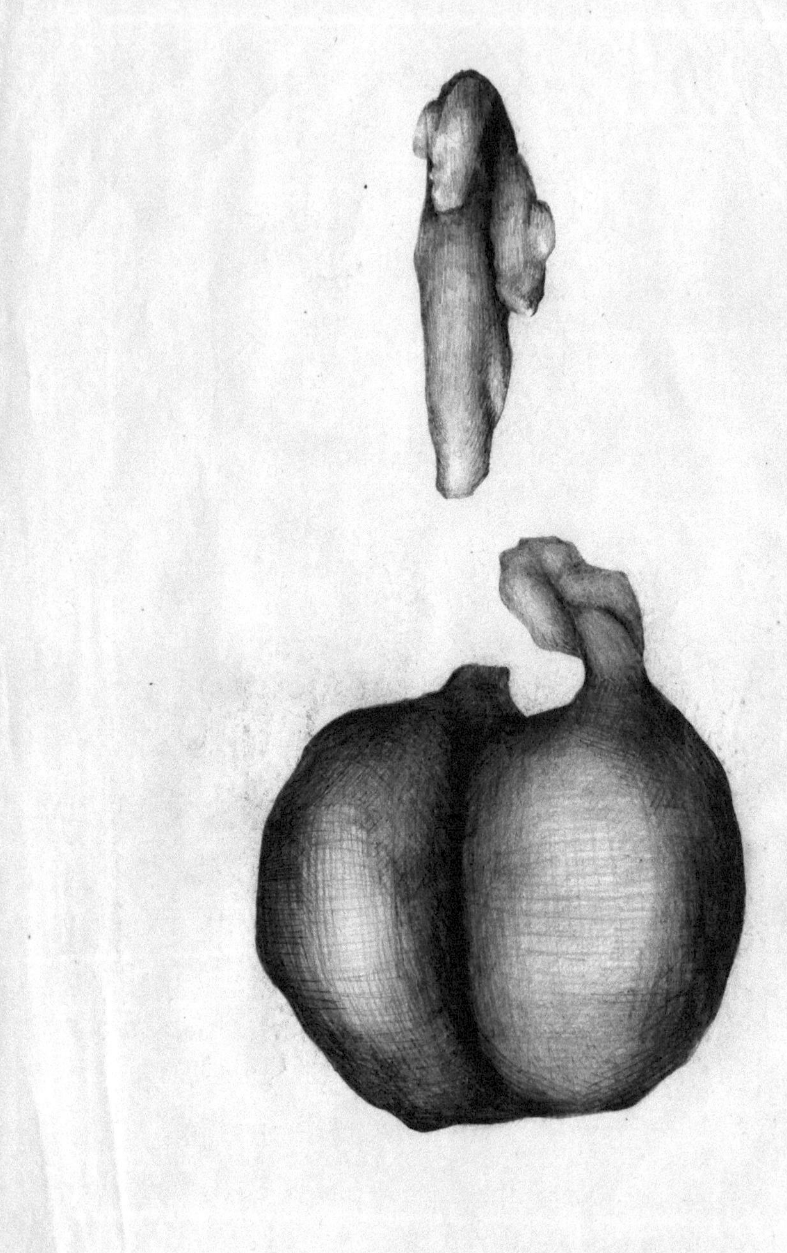

I see so many beautiful women. Walking, talking, seated on the metro. Paris abounds with radiant femmes. The beauties most attractive to me are brunettes. Brown and black haired ladies of various nationalities. I stare with discretion at a well measured distance. These women are neither very young nor old but in their prime. Within moments the cause of my admiration becomes clear. They resemble you. Ofttimes I superimpose your face upon these women. I imagine you.

I quickly become sensual, growing warm, affectionate, love struck for you. I may close my eyes to envision the deep wells of your eyes. Next I draw out your smile. I will call up your voice and listen to your laughter. I then outline and slowly trace your most erotic physique. If I should allow this distraction to continue I reach for the touch of your hand, your shoulder, the nape of your neck. Trancelike I lean forward into your embrace. This is the moment I lose all sense of my intended destination as I am rendered helpless before the image of you.

. . .

. . .

There is no vacuum between lovers. This is the intangible law of love. I am in a timeless space, consumed by throbbing sensations, romantic desires. I have entered an ethereal mist of delightful fragrance most uniquely yours. Vertigo sends me reeling, absent the confines of floor, walls and ceiling. I have escaped gravity's hold, afloat in weightless abandon, a state of absolute comfort, safe and secure from doubt and reservation, enjoined to the love that is you.

Mere mortal I am, a bell, a buzzer, the shriek of the brakes returns me to my task at hand. I step from the metro, exit through a door to feel the slap of a cold winter rain to my face. At this juncture your presence is indelibly stamped to my heart. Alone I need no word or sight of you, no palpable contact. The proof of my love is stowed unshakable in the deep reserve of me, reserved for you. From this wellspring you flow fluid, flush, circulating throughout my body, through my limbs, in my mind's eye, part and parcel of the breaths I give out.

Comes the late hour and I have done all that I could do since I began this journey. I let go the routines, the acts to prepare for sleep. Last on my mind, in my wandering thoughts, would it please you to know? I have carried you along in the pockets of my day.

2.

3 A.M.

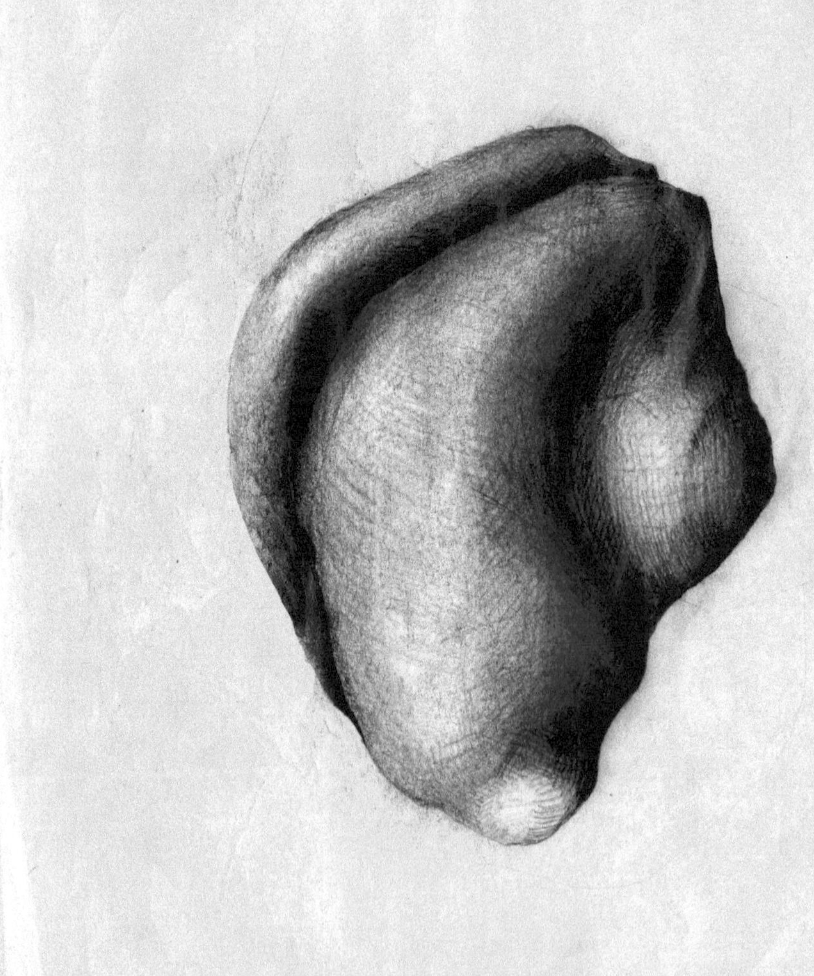

The rains came at the hour of deep sleep for some, restless turns repeating conflicts for others. The darkest hour, when death calls for those worn to fade away.

At 3 a.m. the rains fell upon Paris, syncopated beat-beat-beat, splash on thirsty stone, uncountable measures in percussion taps my window pane. All the while a dormant cloak wraps itself around the city, prostrate, taken, its eyes closed.

Window open I lean to breath the humid musk, touch of nocturne dew. A man coughs up his nightly phlegm. An old woman wrestles her portal closed, secure against the weather, safe from absolutely nothing. She drowns away in the empty vessel of herself.

Two young lovers down below. His husky voice calls "is there more wine?" I reply by faint whisper, the bottle, empty. It fills your head, levitating your restless whims, your swollen head. Lie, be still. Your lover's bed, a lullaby coo softly spoken. Now take to sleep or if you prefer, take a plunge with your lover. Gaze through the darkness to the light in her eyes and say, how beautiful you are, beautiful your love, beautiful life on the edge of night, turning to a morning promise. Rain pouring, wetting the world of both of us. All that we need, everything near, all that we seek, touch and be here, with the night and its rain all surround. An old man dies, a child is born, we balance into each other, all is right. When we fall to passion's call, fatigue of pleasure, a day complete in the solitude of two. Let it sleep. Beat-Beat-Beat from heart to head. Free fall into dream.

3.

A VOICE

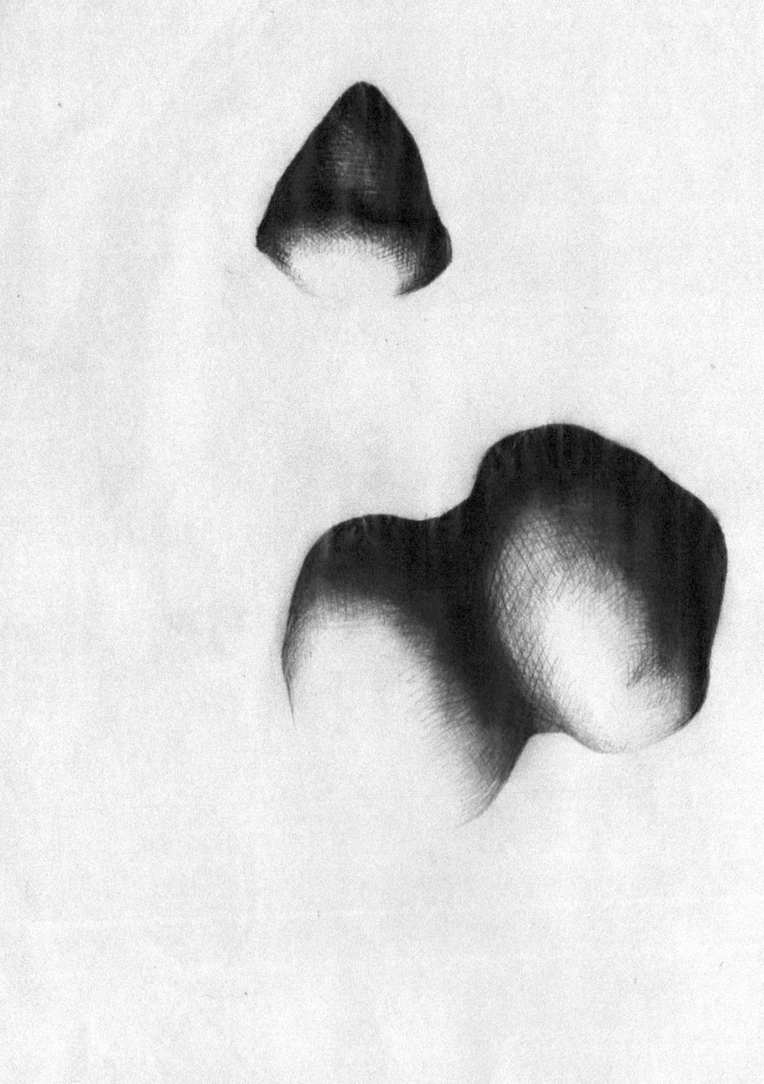

I hear your voice. Sweet and soft. Your breath, gentle upon my cheek. Your hand at rest upon my chest. We have experienced an act of thoroughly satisfying love making. The room now quiet. The world now still. Calm settles upon us like a satin sheet. We have arrived to a state of graceful relaxation. We have joyously tired ourselves in tonic duet. We have fed each other on love and passion. We are satiated. All is given, all received. Our breathing takes the cadence of a restful tide. Our hearts beat to the rhythm of the earth. Our blood flows with the underground stream. In silence, mysterious in its revelation, in soothing darkness we know happiness. By emptying ourselves we are made complete. Each in oneself, one for the other. Delicately you press your lips to my ear and whisper, "I love you". I smile and reply in kind, "I love you". We pause. A sacred presence fills the air between and within us. We are wrapped in this. Union. Two halves joined. Vibrations, the ring of our two-part harmony elevated to the sixth sense. Sleep follows cloaked in tenderness known to they who have completed the wonderful act of sharing one of life's greatest marvels; an act of love beyond description. All we need, need know, to reach for tomorrow, is within us. Promise fulfilled. Life renewed. Awesome in its beauty.

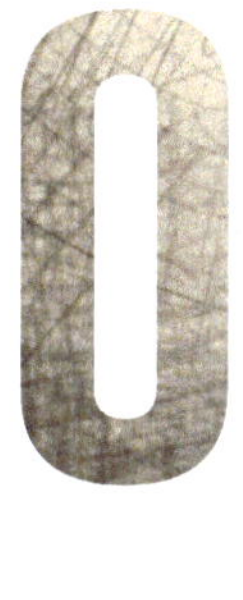

OBLIVION MAGIC

Unity
Bread to the mouth
Milk to the lips
Tongue to the nipple
Tender loin bathes
In the honey of your hive
Tender pleasures our lives
Separate and shared
Under my sun, your moon
Round as butt cakes
Cupped in my hands
Yours upon my cheeks
Descending
Deep wells of your eyes
Fires of orgasm and prayer
Burning us
Death for rebirth
We give one to another
That we may lie
And rise again
Horizons broad
As curved shoulders
We clutch with melting fingers
The final moment
Letting go
Everything
Precious
This
Life
Gives
Us
Such
Short
Time

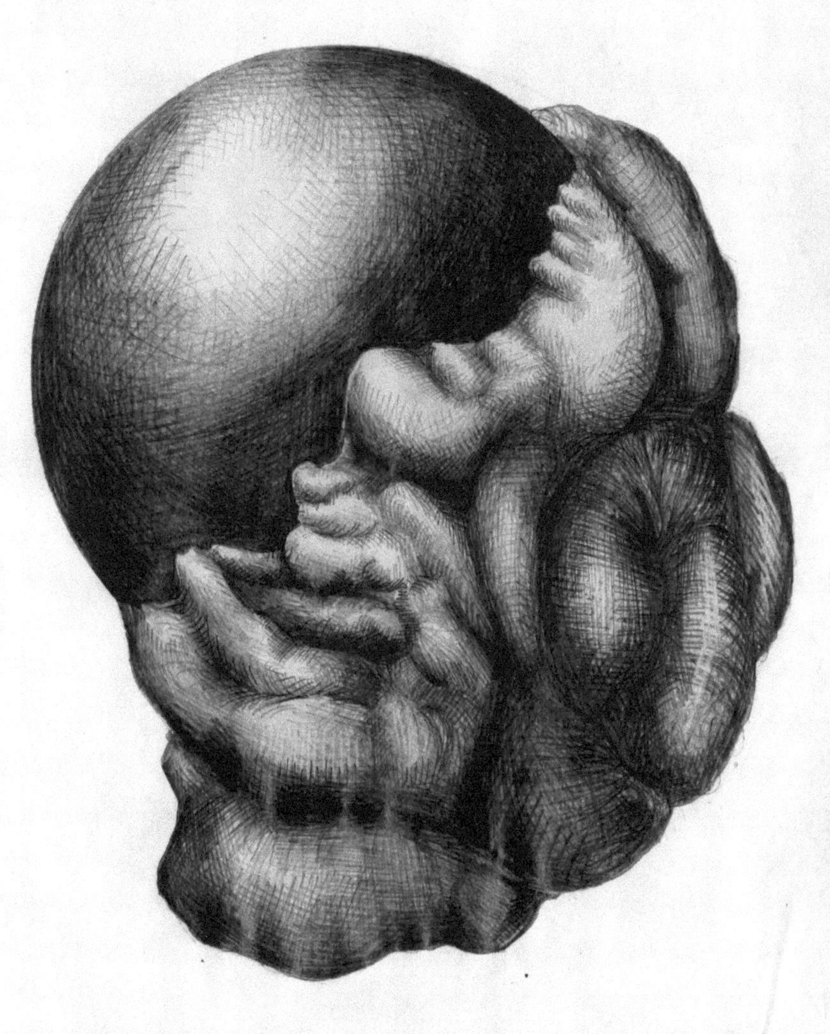

Clitoris

YOUR KISS

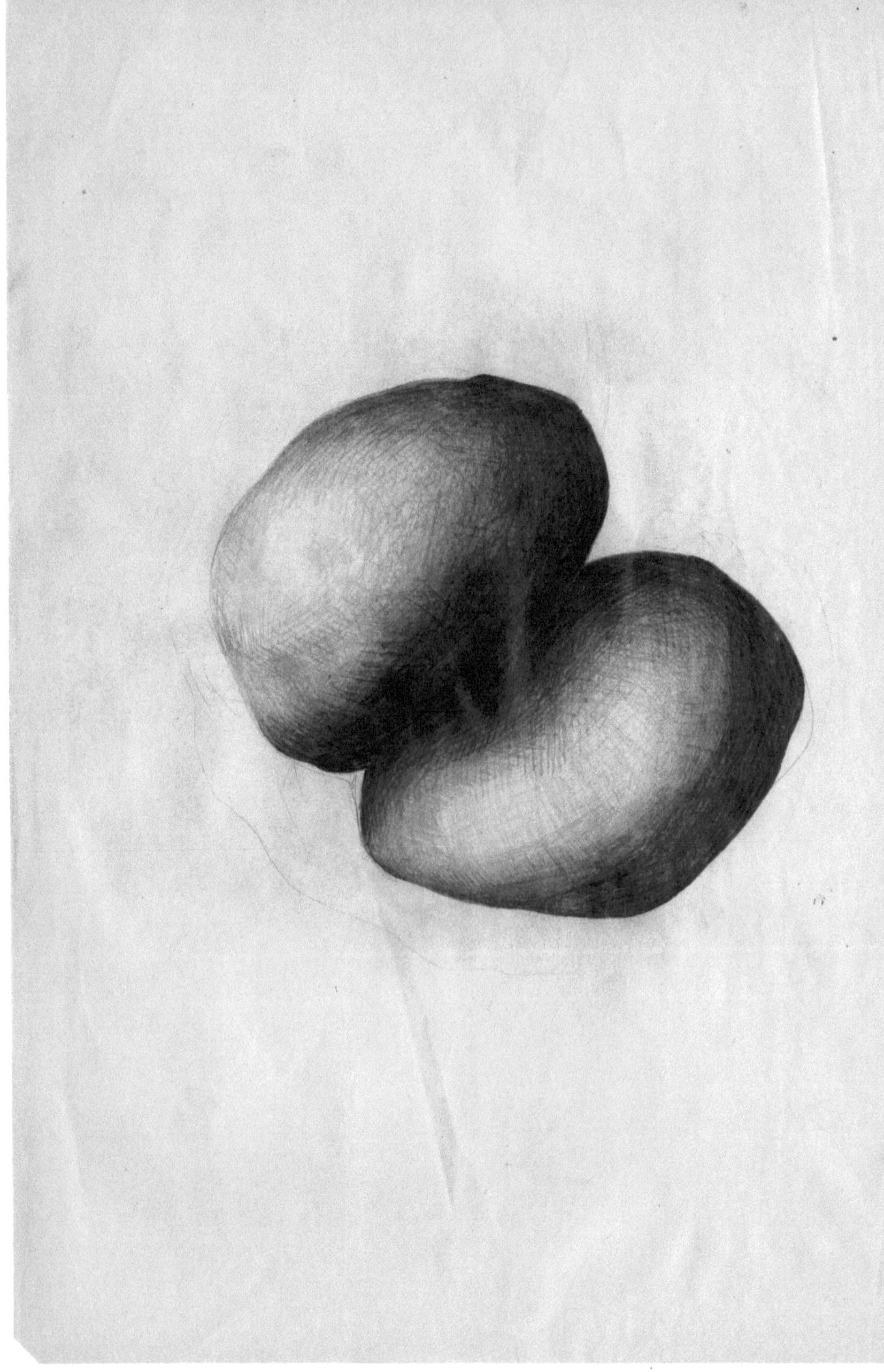

Your kiss shot through me like
A heat seeking missile fixed on pleasure
Your breath fanned my flame
The blood in my tongue caught fire
Your kiss put back the light in my eyes
I am shining and bright
I see the road home in the centuries of stone
A thousand years have passed
And still I know you by your touch, taste, and your smell

Our embrace pleased fickle Paris such
She paused to star light smile
She blew a perfumed breeze
And filled the air with wind song

Your kiss solved mysteries
Stirred in my vague dreams
Of exile across sands of time
And adrift in the sea of solitude
Under midnight skies
I sang your song in the darkness

Your kiss is ageless
Its taste of herbs and oils
A balm to my lips
Salve to my soul

. . .

. . .

Your kiss was brief
And you soon gone
I stand alone
Upon the rock of ages
Where river spills into her ocean
Spellbound, still, I let go
The dam of my desires
Bursts of bittersweet streams
Waltz upon the waves

I love you so this Sunday night
A fool enlightened, a poet driven
To the brink of beautiful sorrow

The coming dawn shall feel the sun
Gently press his lips upon
The quiet nocturne surrenders all

SYLVIA'S SONG

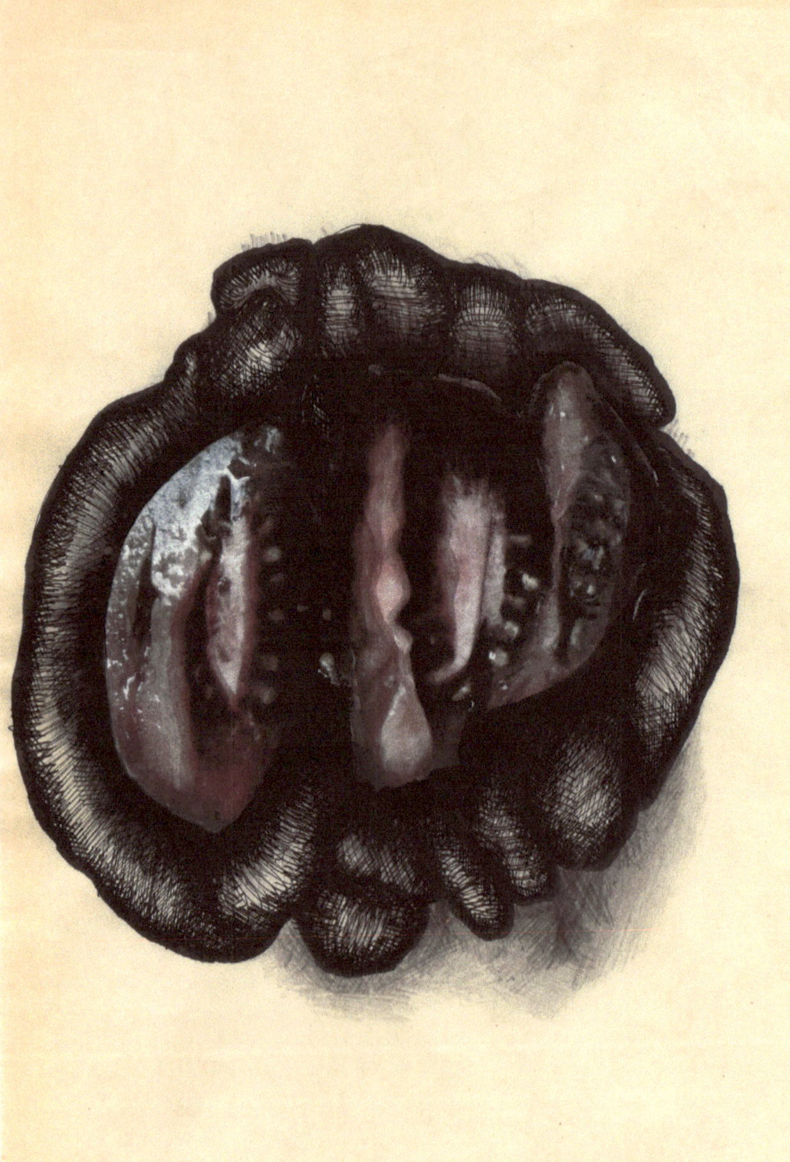

Dear Sylvia,

I wish you to know how many evenings, slipping into nocturne, twilight dusk, a gray shadow merging into violet, I trek to the club, to hear my favorite singer. I seek more than entertainment, more than art for arts sake. I come looking, listening for consummate satisfaction. Jazz.

I need raucous laughs and then some. I fill with glee generated by one who feels the funny side of blue, who bares from inside out, a genuine smile. A woman whose giggle and chuckle is what we emit as breath of life. Nobody laughing at each other, but with each other. Call it medicinal. Call it vitamin vivant. Your jokes, relaxing. Your smile, intoxicating. Bring it home.

You, a stunning example of a beautiful woman, a beautiful voice. Elegant. Eloquent. I need to hear you sing the songs of my restless mind, my troubled soul, stir my soft, so tender center. Songs of love and love lost. Songs conveying a message. A beacon of hope. Resolve in the face of despair. We stay in the game against the odds. Beauty is stubborn.

You're a woman whose charisma is forged from the fires of trials and try again. I need to hear—night time is the right time and the right time is now! This is musical Zen.

I thrive on testimony. Redemption transmitted on voice waves, amplified calls of my scattered family. Me, a stranger in a strange land, no longer estranged. Born again, birthed in the sweet and bitter sweet notes of the ancestors whose legacies flow on the melodic phrase of your wail and coo. Spellbinder, your moans and groans trigger a simultaneous release throughout the crowd. You belt out notes from the primal code of the human race.

Harmony.

. . .

. . .

I want it known, I walk toward dawn through empty nights, full of vigor, humming phrases you have sung hours earlier. You were here and I was present then, now. Sing lady sing, «In the Dark». I glide home weightless on twined hued lights of silver and onyx. Against menacing cold your songs wrap me warm. I kiss your lips, imagination enough. Human Being Human. I carry these little things in the pockets of my day, and nights. Charms.

This poet realizes this state precedes language. It being murmurs of heart, beat of the the soul in step with a turning planet shuffling its way through the cosmos of mysteries and wonders. What could this moment be named? Magic.

You are a gift. In exchange for your value I offer the currency of my immeasurable admiration.

Baby, you shake the diamonds from the diamond dust.

In the spirit,
Moe Seager

(dedicated to Sylvia Howard, Paris diva)

PERHAPS

Morning gives to afternoon
Time to tuck away dreams, desires, inner being
Corporeal gravity to transparent routines, anemic rituals
Rain. Spring returns from exile
Sucks on April's nipples

Thunder claps, lightning flash
Fear and falling waters
Herd us against each other
Repelling most in hurried flight for home
Where we are absolutely safe
From nothing
Witness those drowning
In the empty vessels of themselves

Oh this day would be dull, boring
Were it not for the occasional flash
Of bright umbrellas
One—the color red
To remind us
We are

My umbrella is a tent
I a nomad
Wandering through this village
Not quite sure of how to conduct myself

By chance, design?
We come upon each other
Relief
The solitude of two

Too soon it is time
You must go
I shall wait
Beauty is stubborn

Perhaps it will rain tomorrow

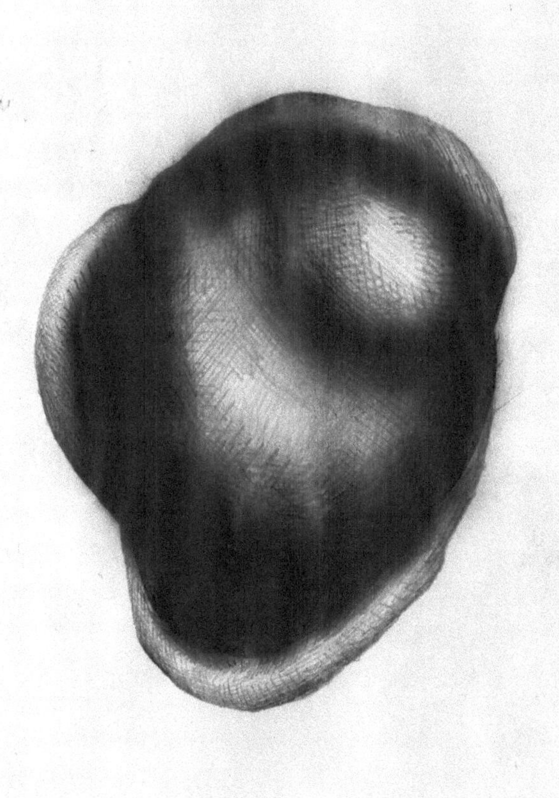

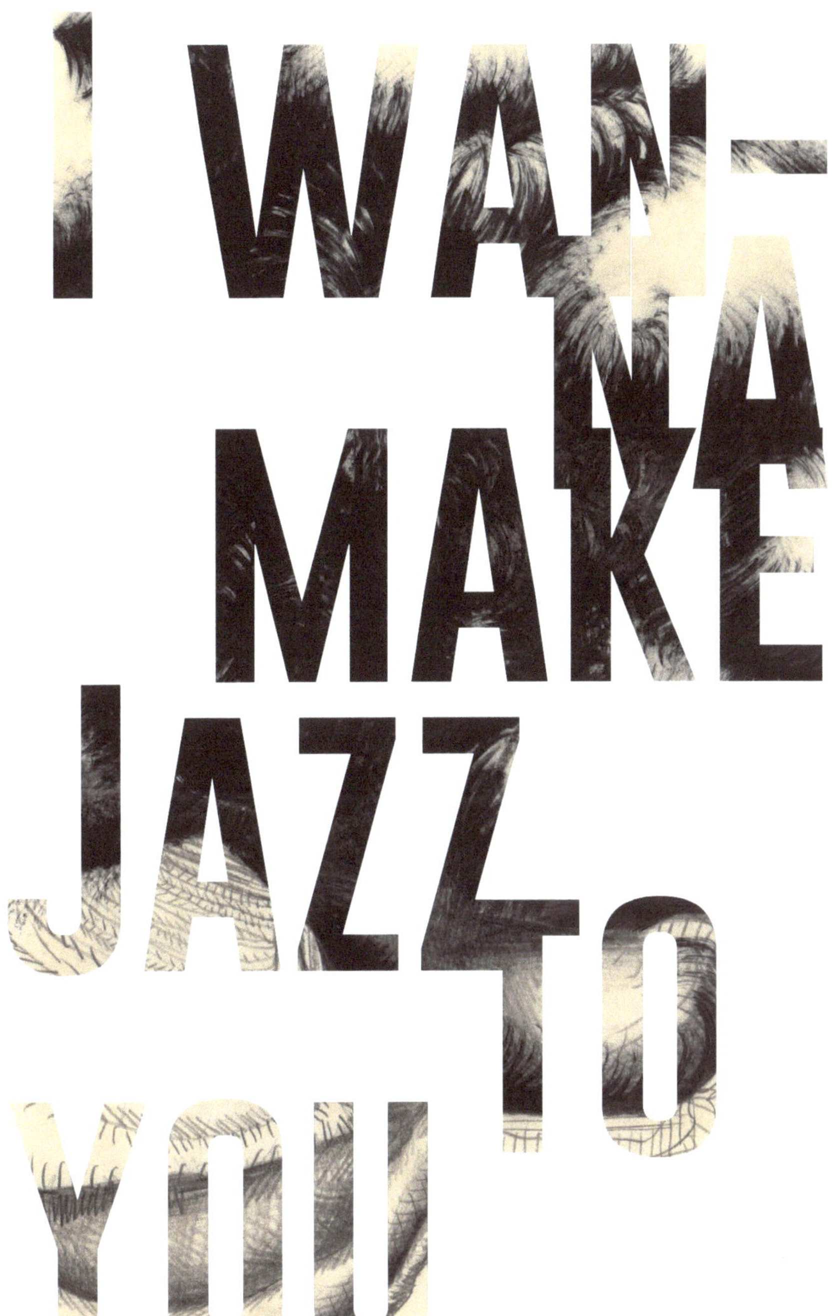
I WAN-
NA
MAKE
JAZZ
TO
YOU

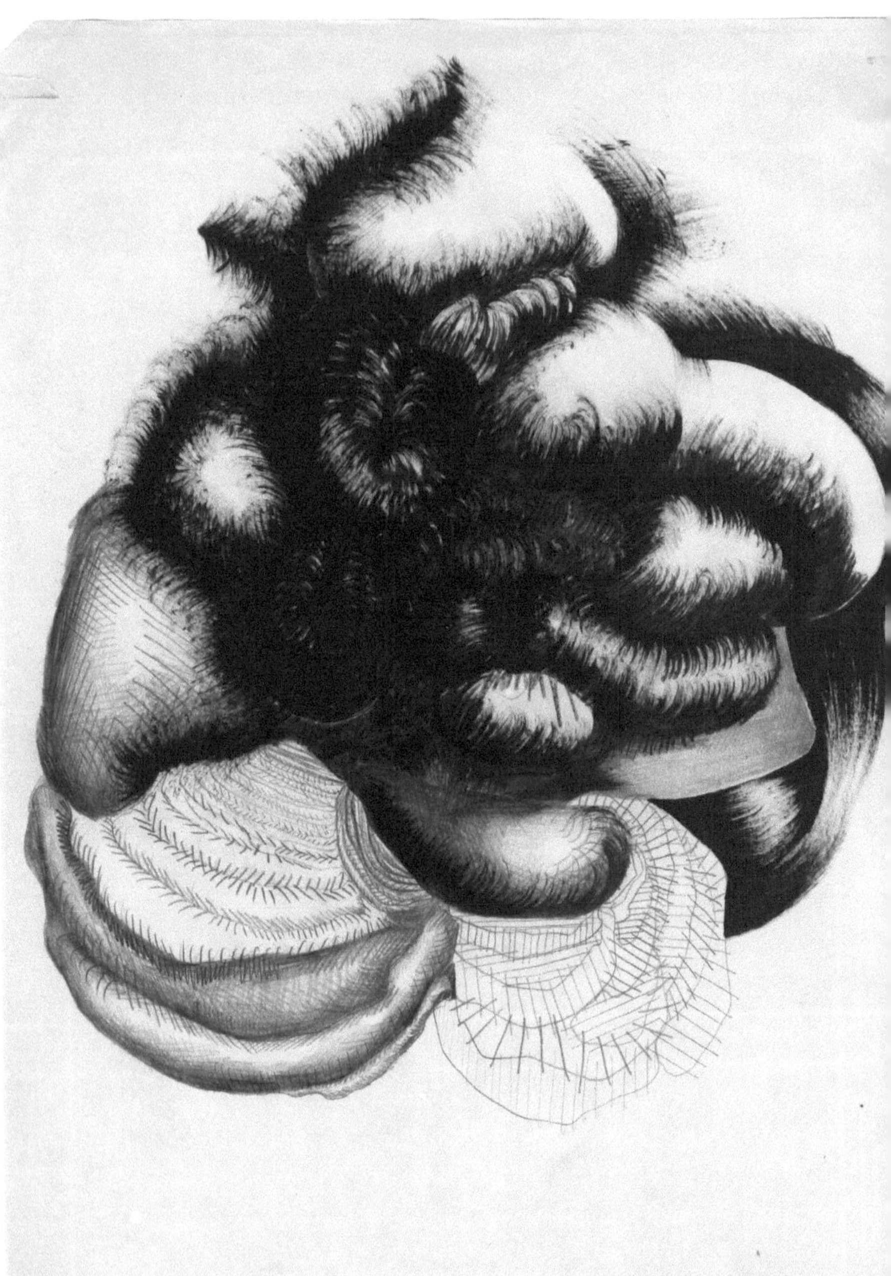

We started out on a walk
In step, in time
We found a lot
To share, to find
The two of us
So smooth our groove
I wanna make jazz with you
I wanna make jazz to you

Pretty soon we got the beat and key
Trading notes in melody
Right away we found the stroke, didn't we
We took the count way out, yes we
I wanna make jazz with you
I wanna make jazz to you

Through the night we learned to play, okay
We got it on, on and on, got it off our way
We found our song, our harmony
We carried on from dusk till dawn, oh please
I wanna make jazz with you
I wanna make jazz to you

> *You pluck the strings*
> *I'll blow the horn*
> *We gotta song to sing*
> *Baby, this child's born*

Our repertoire, it amazes me
So deep and down, our possibilities
Include a take I never dreamed was there
I never felt so rich, so rare
We took the risk, we beat the dare
Dare I say
I wanna make jazz with you
I wanna make jazz to you

Let's make this riff our last tune tonight
A private encore, so, cut the light
I wanna be bop all the pitch you got
I wanna jam it till you wail and drop
I wanna play it, I gotta say it
Baby please don´t stop
I wanna make jazz with you
I wanna make jazz to you

You pluck the strings
I'll blow the horn
We gotta song to sing
Baby, this child´s born

I wanna make jazz with you
I wanna make jazz to you

WASTED TIME AT THE BOOK-STORE

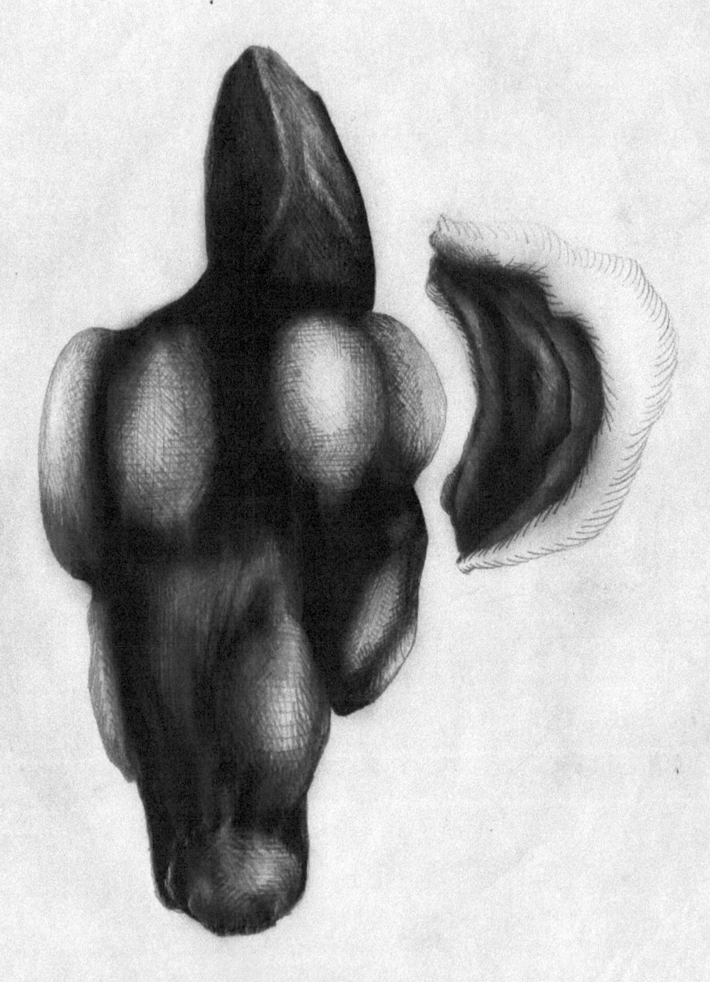

The girl wants to be heard.
I guess so. She talks a lot.
None of you guys will listen.
She's just . . . I don't know man.
You don't know women either.
What's that supposed to mean?
Why not ask her.
She's too uptight.
She didn't fuck you?
She doesn't fuck anybody.
Yes, she does.
Okay, who?
Guys who listen.
What are you saying?
Are you listening?
Yes.
Your mother had aspirations.
You mother fucker!
Your father was a bludgeon.
You are crazy.
So is she.
Who?
She with ideas.
I don't understand?
I know.

BLUE
BONNET
GIRL

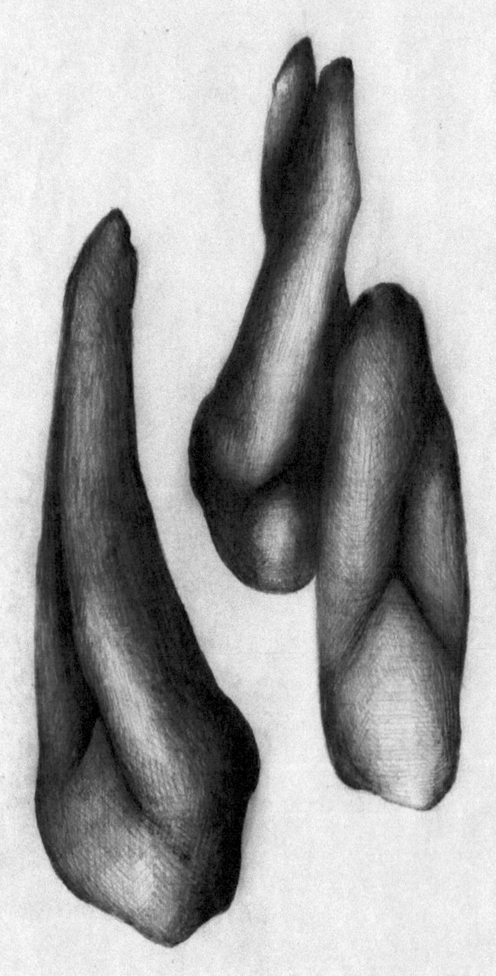

The sun comes up, I'm lying down
Alone in bed, the only sound
Your lazy laughter bouncing round
My head, and last night parting

I must have dropped a funny line
I'm good for a joke, most any old time
I hide my shy side in my eyes
Now honey, that's no joking matter

Was trying to fool you, so you wouldn't see
A lonely drifter, that's not me
I'm good time Charley, down with the plan
Wrap your soft self round this hard shell man

I know you told me, just one dance
Two times dizzy round the party hall
And had us a coffee, on Sunday noon
I talked too much, you left too soon

I'll take you out in your home town
You make me out the best you can
We'll step on guitar chords, a fretless bass
Fretful times in a world gone mad

(chorus)
Cowboys and cowgirls, hip city pips
You from the pine woods, I'm brick alley slick
To meet up in Austin, a dream I got lost in
I'll be your main man, you be my miss
All the world's getting bigger as we hold on close
Your poet, your singer, I'll jump through the ropes
For a little bitty smile from your pretty pink lips
Blue Bonnet girl, my brown eyed miss

. . .

. . .

I called you to ask if maybe we could
Walk the river, sing to song birds, soft stones and hard wood
I'd favor you blossoms, turn inward to say
What I could not speak aloud

Maybe it's Texas, the music, the crowd
Motorcycles, my cycle, come forward, come proud
Summon the word, the verve from a cloud
So happy simply to meet you

That I took you out for a night on your town
Shared a cold beer at Jo's, smoked a j' in the sand
Waved as you drove off, dumbstruck alone
I sang me a love song as I rambled home

My suitcase is sighing, not a suit in the bag
We were good together, but I wouldn't brag
So tall and steady, she at my side
In soon time, she won't remember

(chorus)
Cowboys and cowgirls, hip city pips
You from the pine woods, I'm brick alley slick
To meet up in Austin, a dream I got lost in
I'll be your main man, you be my miss
All the world's getting bigger as we hold on close
Your poet, your singer, I'll jump through the ropes
For a little bitty smile from your pretty pink lips
Blue Bonnet girl, my brown eyed miss

THE ENGA- GEMENT

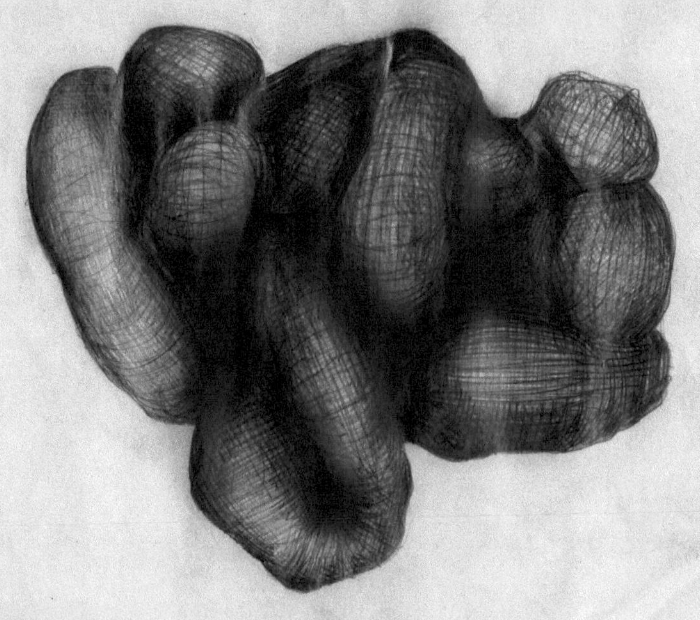

At the bar
It was late
Payday
I was shitfaced

In a booth
She sat
Alone
I got ideas

Poured a drink
Distilled a fantasy
Consumed
In torrid pleasure

Hand in hand
Across the arc
Windblown
Out to sea

By torrent sweats
Of liquid courage
Stumbling
I made my move

In a flash
She erupted
Leper, you need a doctor
I'm not your cure

Crawling back to the bar
'Hey'
She bellowed,
'Guys like you stick their brains
up their asshole
and use their cock as a periscope
Call a charity, you poster child'

. . .

. . .

Everybody
In the joint
Howling

She was tough
A forty pound hammer
Thrown squarely against
A two-penny nail

Downed a double
With a chaser
Humiliated
I replied,
Okay smart shit answer this
Everybody's got a jones
You know mine
What's yours?

Loneliness, she replied
Sound familiar?
I said Hey babe
That's my monkey too

The whole joint froze
We just stared
Til she cracked a grin
I licked my lips
She lit a smoke
You could hear a pin drop

I took a whiskey shot straight up
She got beside me, sat on down
I told the barman sure as shit
Give the lady one more round

I took a whiskey shot straight up
She got beside me, sat on down
I told the barman sure as shit
Give the lady one more round

She bought a six pack
Under her arm
'No harm in walking me
home to my place'

A pinball machine rang loudly
Somebody won the door prize

We strode to the street
Side by side in the dead of night
A stray dog loping
A stray cat stride
River rats haunched
Peering through the fog

BABY'S LUST

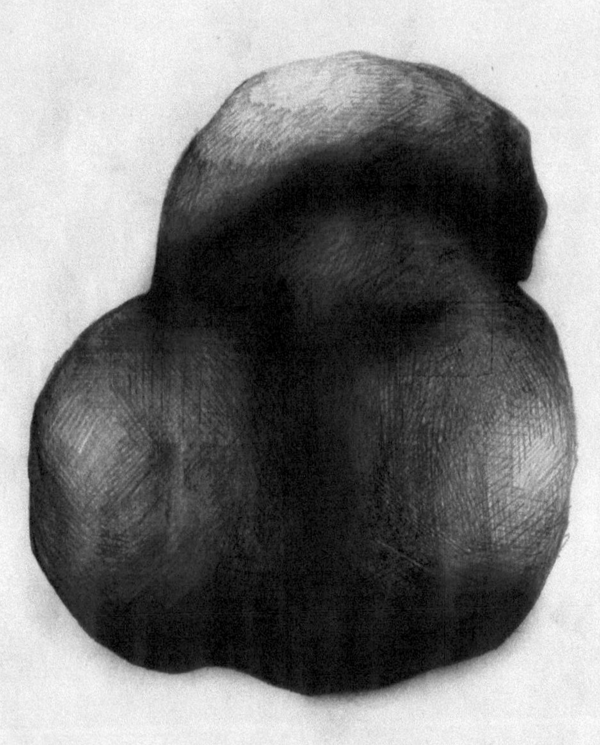

I culled you, my drug of choice
Drank you like fleeting liquor
Mounted you in a fog
Like a needle in my arm

Daydreams repeating themselves
Nights of mindless succession
You carried me through lips and folds
And mounds of flesh
Tucked in your womb, I danced
Song of warm wet chords

One of us, driven by primal hunger
One of us, fetal feeding
Sensual slumber

Like a day exhausted
You turned on your axis
Purging me, breach,
Drunk in my confusion
Mother left me for another man

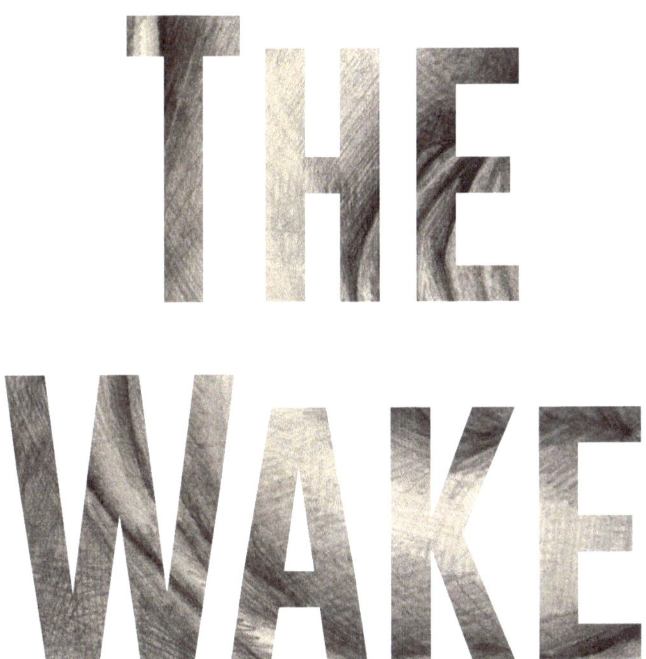
THE
WAKE

Prologue

Did you grip the metal
Grit your teeth
Roll your eyes
Raise the pistol
Put down the pain
Aim point blank
Bullet to the brain

Wait
Did you think of me
Before the squeeze
Sigh of relief
One last laugh
As you let it rip

Joe has died
With him goes a part of me
Where brilliant light flickers
Fades to nothingness
My main man's gone
Committed suicide

Joe had what so many want
Very few possess
Was with Joe
While Joe was here
Here with us

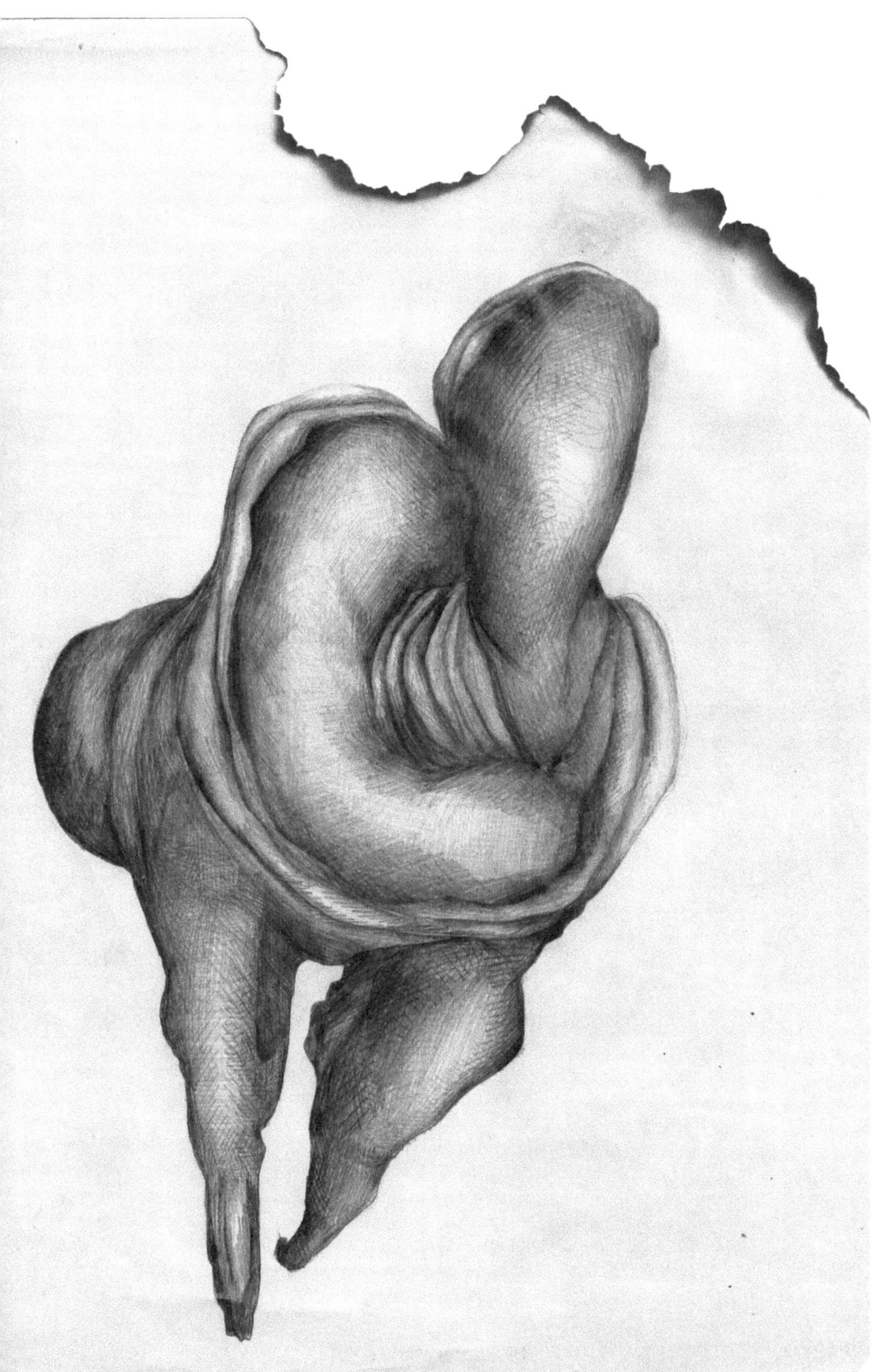

You see Joe
His gifted talk
His funky walk
His stride with pride
Style and flair
All his own
Goddamn beautiful Joe

Oh for the life of me
As cute and bad
As I could be
Most I could do was shadow dance
When that man took the floor

He the daring, dashing North Side prince
I the East End Cinderella fellow
It was a ball

Often we danced with the ladies
Moving in circles
Shoulder to shoulder
Side to side
We were so loose
We were so tight

Caring, sharing, drinking and swearing
To our friends and our fathers alike
Now look here folks
Moey and Joey wish to inform you
We are taking a pause for the cause
My main man gone
Committed suicide

Joe has died
I cried, hear me cry
I have missed a rare moment
One I repressed
Leaning into your pile driving arms
Against that hammer in your chest

Making our getaway
Up we went over the wall
From dead end streets
And deadbeat deeds
The slums and their sums
Of long gone dreams
Choked in a cloud of factory smoke

Gone with him
That gifted talk, that funky walk
I'm canceling Christmas
And the Fourth of July
My main man's gone
Committed suicide

Alone with memories
That prance about the room
It falls on me
Like hot rivets and fly ash
North Side sweaty, salty
Blood stained, steel toed, wet drenched
I can still smell him

Here's to Joe
You marvelous son-of-a-bitch
We had plans man
But you took it on the chin
Who knows, it could have been me

It could have been different
We should have vacationed
Two mates at anchor
A noon day sun
A condor soars
The earth so still
Trouble behind
I'll be the wind
You be the kite

SEDUC-
TRESS

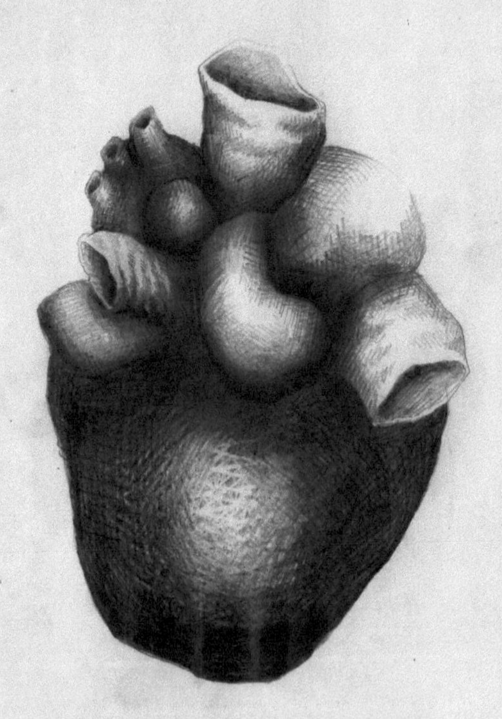

I barreled into Marseilles burning rubber
Double clutching fifth gear on a bottle of red
A bag of smoke spark plugs shooting fire
All tanked up, high octane and blasts
Cuban trumpets leading the charge

Leaning into her porous white rocks
At 80 kilometers an hour
Her walls dancing in our headlights
Like melting candle wax

Her burgundy bay under Lupus lights
Undulating like a Mediterranean woman
Large, dark and saucy
Spreading her waves, spitting her splash
Salty swells lapping the sandstone
Kissing in the mist, humid, wet hot

A terrestrial constellation
Sea serpent snaking the womb of Isabelle
Seamen fishing for clams
The pearls of Marseilles
Make a man want to dive in head first

Along a lover´s labyrinth
We come to the beach of Scorpio's moon
Naked lovers spread on the sands
I see her, I gasp

She is caramel to lick
Her licorice hair, green eyes starlight glossy
Her pony ass curved like the earth that gave her
Rose hips arched like the gates of Troy
Her black cat pussy purrs
Nipples like tender olive skins
You don't spit out —
You suck them.

Dugan and Reilly

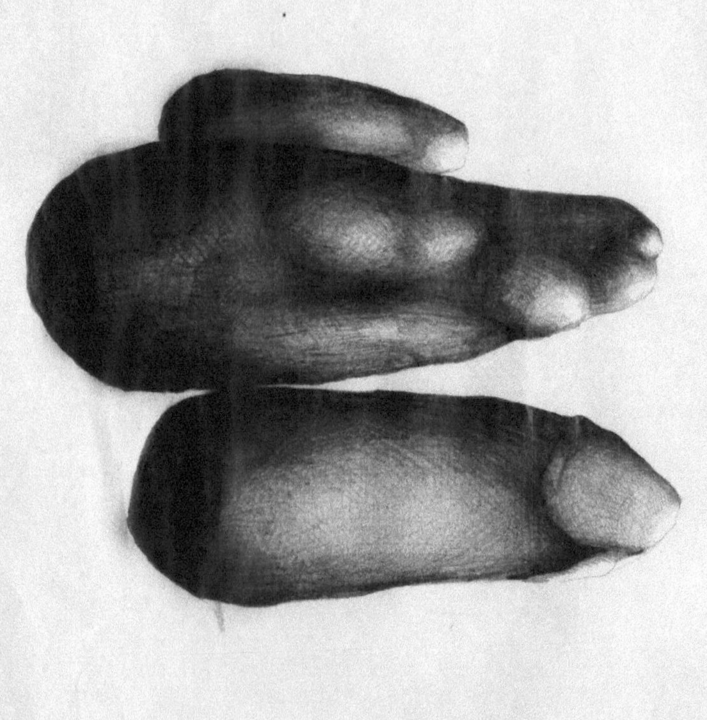

Prologue

I had what?
My best. My worst.
I tried so hard.
I wanted, badly.
But things happen, believe me, things happen.

O.K., it took place in the body.
No, it took place in the mind.
Alright, alright, it happened in my soul.

I was brave.
No, I was a coward.
Tell the truth man, tell the truth.
No more lies, no more lies.

Look, I know what happened.
I know what it was, who he was.
But who was I?
The truth, just the truth.
That's the hard part.

You see, it was a rumble.
It was a dance.
Is there a difference?

It was rivalry. It was jealousy.
It was envy. It was hatred.
It was passion, misguided love.

Tell the truth?
Dare I speak it?
Can I do it?
Set the secret free?

. . .

. . .

It's not what you think.
Not what I thought.
I was afraid, yes, very afraid.
Fear I could not identify.
I would not reveal.

How I felt. About that night.
Every night since.
Every day the world turns on her axis.
I too turn. And twist with it.
A corkscrew snaking from my core.
Winding its way through my ribs, to my neck.
Just beneath the skin. I cover my flesh.
To hide the scars.

I had the strength to knock him backwards
Three full steps with one punch
I had the will to lift myself from the pavement
When he returned the blow
I had the stamina to go ten street rounds
Though I knew I was beaten in the first

Street lights flooded our makeshift ring
Neon flashing on and off in cadence
With the terrible thumping over my left eye
When he landed a hammer shot
Lightning, then thunder

. . .

Neon flashing on and off
The clammy sheen of our skins
Blood drops dripping through a haze of perspiration
The vital juices we gave, like there was no tomorrow

A crowd stood around us
I saw through swollen eyes
Their gasps, awes, mimicking
The fierceness of our spectacle
The beastly nature of ourselves

Alone, lonely men lost
Shadow boxing our way through
The prime of our time
Afraid the true reflections
Of ourselves we might see
Mirror image of a lower order

Does my neighbor feel the same sorrow, the same loss
Does he not feed on the same stew,
run from the same shadows
Hide in the same shame, cry in a dark corner

A jagged line of pain rushed through my lungs
Sweat collected in a torn nostril
Acrid as a smelling salt, the shock
Returned to the scene
We were clutching, no, holding each other
Locked we were, in awkward embrace

I slipped from his grip
Flinging both hands against his chest
I squeezed him by his shoulders
Peered through his gaze
Deep into his eyes, there I found him

Exhaustion rose like a fog, saturating head and limb
Adrenaline enough to stand knockkneed, unsteady
Neurons fired wildly, arms flailed aimless
The hammers of our fists, now dead weights
We had given face to save face

A forearm to my ribs sent me stumbling backwards
Against the meat market window
Flush to the glass I slid
Catching a glimpse of myself in the slow descent
In grey silhouette, a picture pathetic
Spartacus in the salt mine

We had lost the crowd
Feeling robbed of a climax
In cold indifference they walked away
Denying a gladiator his last hurrah
Left to ourselves, and a few gawking pigeons
Who soon took flight for a vacant eave
They huddled together as the rain came down

For the sake of reputation, we charged each other
He, a wounded stag, I, a bludgeoned bull
Each brute attempting a decisive blow
Dull thud met with dull thud
We tumbled to the pavement clinging to each other
Lest one man appear the loser

Panting hot, dry heaves in each other's faces
I smelled the onions of his dinner
He smelled the garlic of mine
I, stained with his sweat, he, with my blood
Fused we were, tangled,
our futile moves to come undone
As a bus stopped, the driver bellowed
'Why don't you clowns call it a night'

With cause to pause, I recalled Achilles' bout with Hector
Costumes now different, weapons have changed
Armor once worn on the outside, now inside ourselves
Hero worship unabated throughout the ages
The sole manner by which to distinguish oneself from the mob
A defiant stand in the arena

This brawl, like the duel pitting Achilles upon Hector
A cloaked flirtation played out in warrior dance
Stubborn respect, latent admiration, perverse compassion
For the greater pains, deeper sorrows, within and throughout
Our dismal young lives, too frightening to admit,
taboo to reveal
Truth buried in a vow of silence

Pretending, alleging, it's done for the girl,
some other rare pearl
Helen of Troy, Helen of the East End
We speed our lives away in swift Chevy chariots,
roaring through the gates
Daring the odds, headlong we race, the awaiting brick wall
Savage, so noble, what little we have, we throw away

His grunt returned me to the quiet and calm
I stared at his naked face, mine was the same
A foreign emotion welled within me
An urge to dab my finger, to stop the blood
Flowing from his lower lip
How dogs lick clean their wounds
And those of another

Our eyes locked in such unease
Each searching the other for a sign, a gesture
A solution, relief, an honorable ending
I desperately wanted up and out, but
I didn't have the courage, to call it quits
To lie passively, arms dropped at my sides
I could not forget Achilles' bout with Hector

With cause to pause, I recalled Achilles' bout with Hector
Costumes now different, weapons have changed
Armor once worn on the outside, now inside ourselves
Hero worship unabated throughout the ages
The sole manner by which to distinguish oneself from the mob
A defiant stand in the arena

This brawl, like the duel pitting Achilles upon Hector
A cloaked flirtation played out in warrior dance
Stubborn respect, latent admiration, perverse compassion
For the greater pains, deeper sorrows, within and throughout
Our dismal young lives, too frightening to admit, taboo to reveal
Truth buried in a vow of silence

Pretending, alleging, it's done for the girl, some other rare pearl
Helen of Troy, Helen of the East End
We speed our lives away in swift Chevy chariots, roaring through the gates
Daring the odds, headlong we race, the awaiting brick wall
Savage, so noble, what little we have, we throw away

His grunt returned me to the quiet and calm
I stared at his naked face, mine was the same
A foreign emotion welled within me
An urge to dab my finger, to stop the blood
Flowing from his lower lip
How dogs lick clean their wounds
And those of another

Our eyes locked in such unease
Each searching the other for a sign, a gesture
A solution, relief, an honorable ending
I desperately wanted up and out, but
I didn't have the courage, to call it quits
To lie passively, arms dropped at my sides
I could not forget Achilles' bout with Hector

We lay motionless, clutching each other
Not a word spoken, not a signal, nor a jest given
Speechless I implored, we can take off our armor
Drenched in blood, sweat, soaked with rain, we will surely rust
Getting to him was getting at me

At last I pulled away, shouting, Listen Dugan
I seen big men twice our size
Fall to machines, ground out as pulp
Spit back, teeth, bones and all
Some men share tennis, some men share golf
Our kind share fox holes, at war with the other,
at war with themselves

Startled, he released his grip, so did I
He rose to his feet, shook his shoulders,
Blinked several times and let out a sigh
In a low, deliberate voice he hissed
Reilly, you're an asshole
He turned and walked away

I laughed quietly and murmured
Let's go for a swim, try a new dance
I like the way you wear a hat
He was still in earshot when I shouted
Hey Dugan, see ya around
He shot back, Yeah, see ya around, not anytime soon, OK
Signal and return signal
All was put to normal

Me, I just sat a while
Senseless and stupid for spending myself
On bloodletting and onion breath on a good Friday night
My best suit of armor riddled with dents, cracked at the seams

The rain picked up
I took the back streets and alleys
I cut through the churchyard of Saint Peter and Paul
Taking shelter from the downpour at the house of the Lord

I wondered what young father Michael would make
Of our combat, the violence,
the hurt and the pain we so readily gave
I supposed he would say as he has in times past
From the height of his lofty pulpit, at nine o'clock mass
Men are corrupted, the holy spirit brings peace

To which I'd surely rebut
I live in the world of men
It is among them I seek peace
Can you summon this spirit here to the streets
To break down man made walls, our living hell
This spirit you conjure as a dove
Can it fly with salt on its tail, with blood in its eye

Closer to home I thought about love
Loving my brother, loving myself
How strong the conviction
How much heart muscle it would take
What a better world it could be
My life, your life, the lives we could shape

Just about then the terrible thumping returned
Over my left eye, where he hit me
When I knew I was beaten in the first
But would not surrender, as a wiser man
I didn't have the courage
Did not have the courage

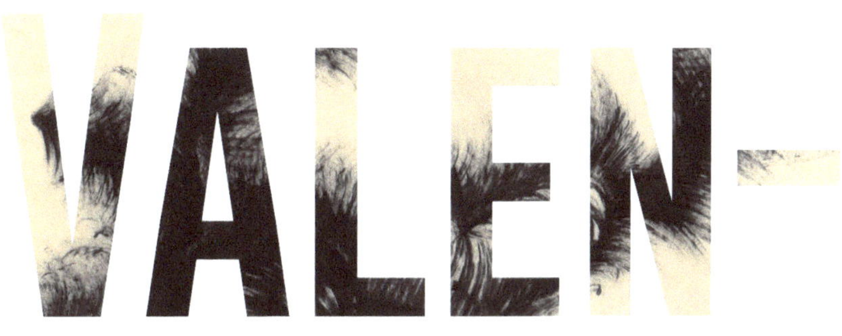

TINE'S
ORACLE

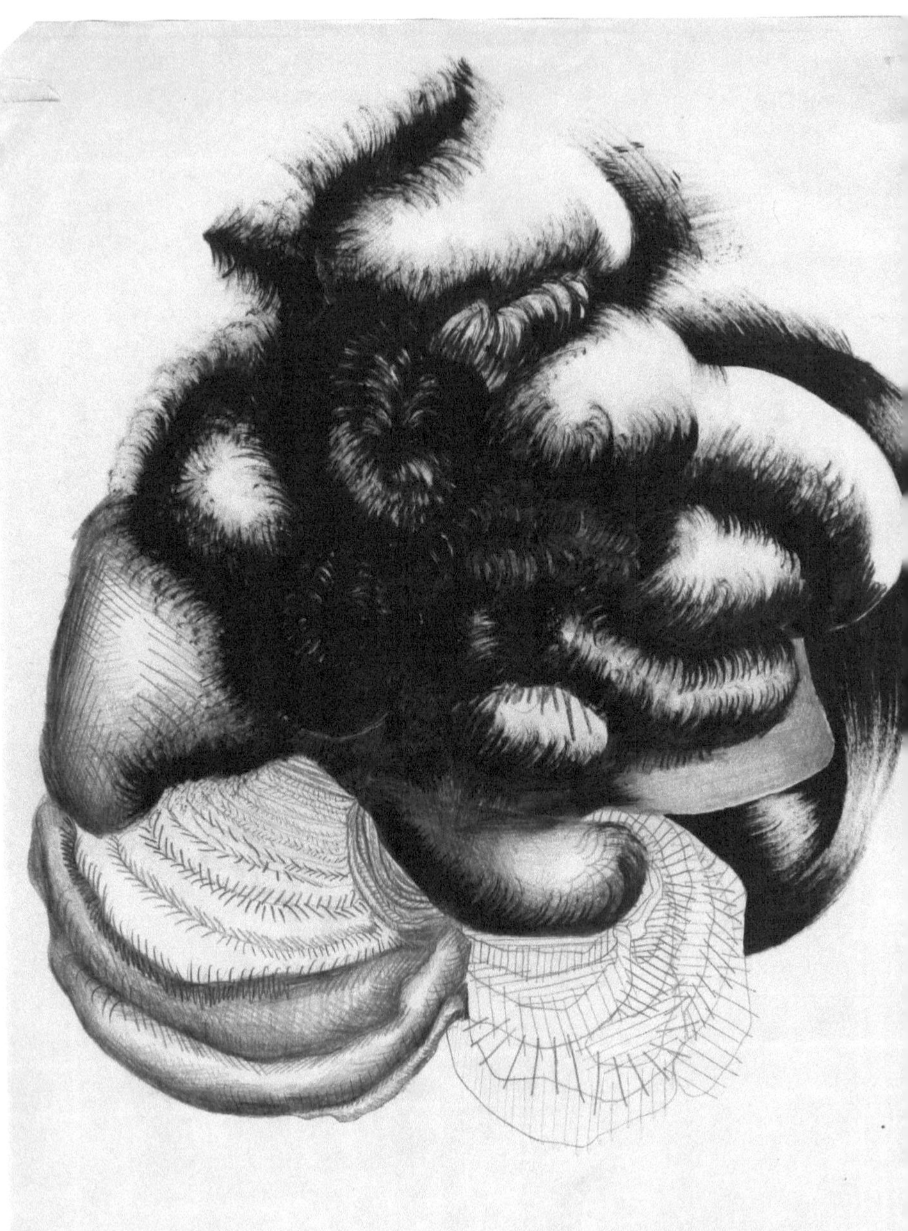

From below I watch you
Standing atop the knob
Of a snow powdered knoll
A full moon rising behind
Its night shine drapes you
In luminescent silver glow

This celestial background
Tracing your small form
Your smooth lines, slight curves
Delicate, fragile, rare

I track stars blue to white
Poking through the blackness
One makes an arc close behind you
Takes my breath away

You wear nocturne's pearls
As dangling ornamental jewelry
In such antediluvian symmetry
You have eclipsed Luna

A fleshly classic figurine
Stands between the earth and sky
About you all else pales to not
You are the visceral center of the universe

HERE

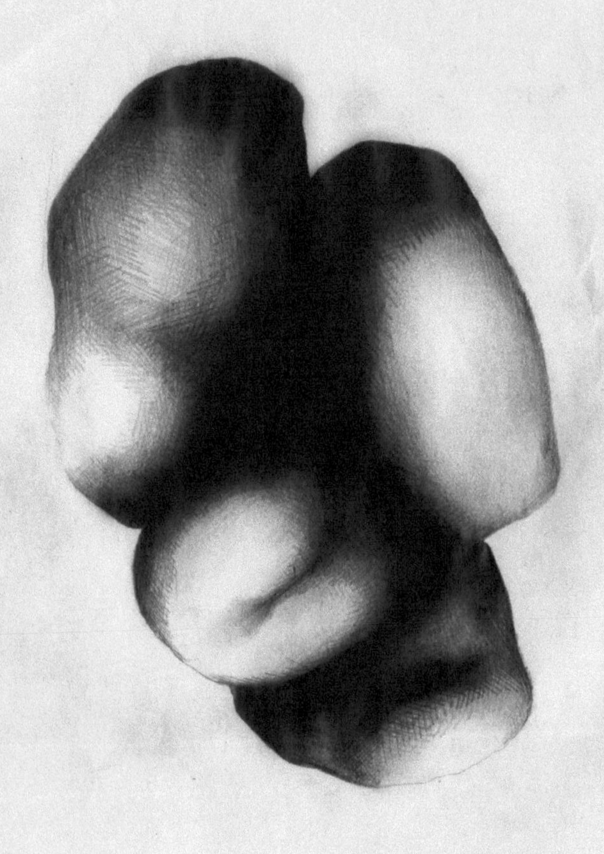

Here
Take it
Place it
In the palm of your hand
Sleep on it
Dream

Here
Does not require
Nor oblige
The meaning
Of this act
Its reward
Light to your soul
And I sing
Your song
And smile

Here
Freely given
Freely received
Feast your eyes
The spark of life
The mystery

Here
It comes
It goes
It wants
Your touch

. . .

Here
Be
Whole
Now
Ever
Yours

Here
Remember
Me
Here
When you
Need
A wave to
Ride on

One
Precious
Drop
of
Life

Here
One
Moment
Bliss
Weightless
Love

■

www.ingramcontent.com/pod-product-compliance
Lightning Source LLC
LaVergne TN
LVHW052253100826
845147LV00001B/32

* 9 7 8 0 9 9 5 6 2 2 5 1 7 *